MW00444949

The

ULTIMATE ADULT COLORING BOOK FOR MEN

2nd Edition

Volume I

** Color test page at back of book

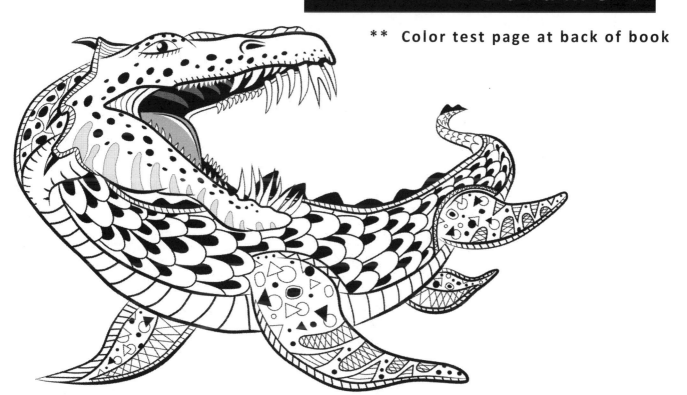

The back of each coloring page has a black backing to provide added protection against ink bleeding.

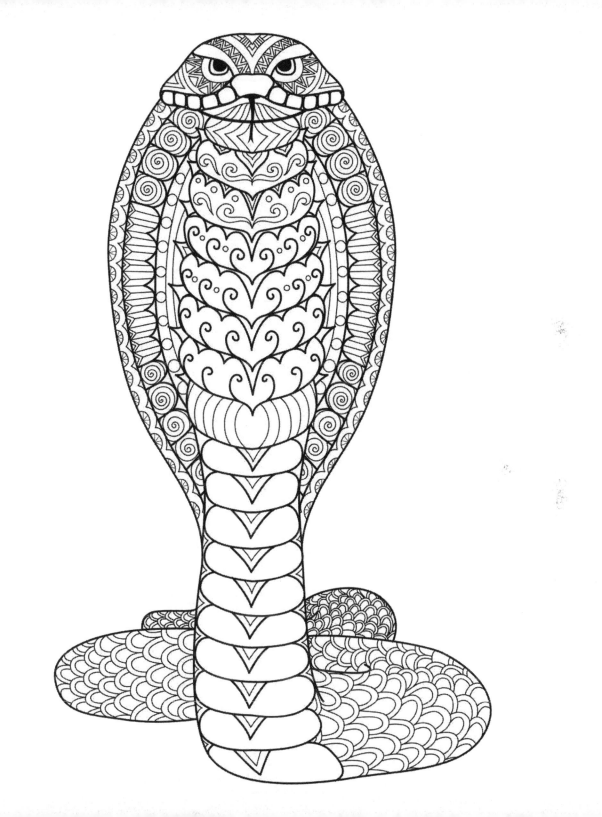

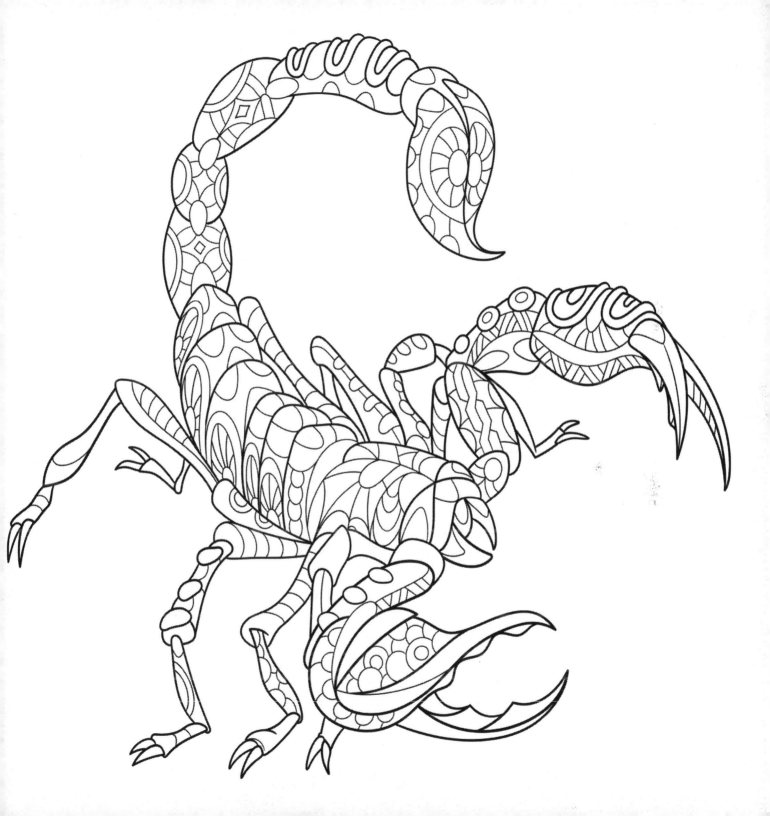

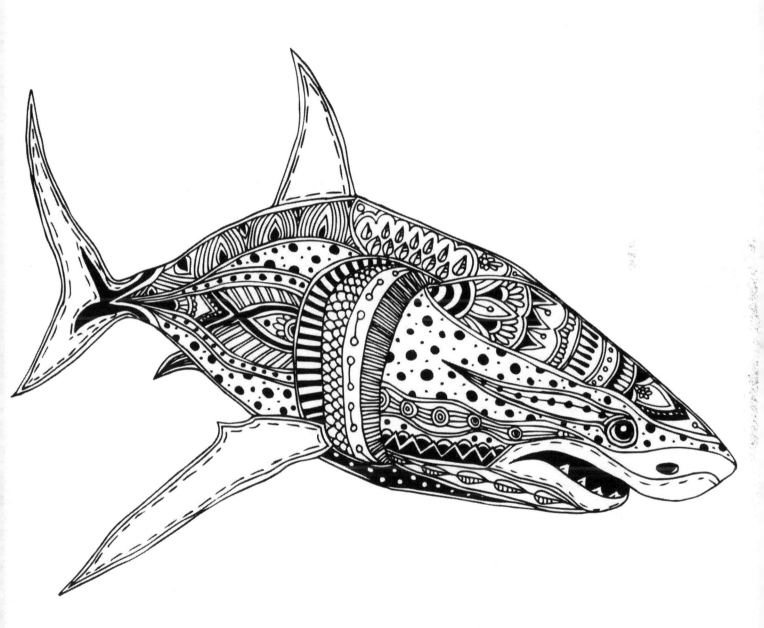

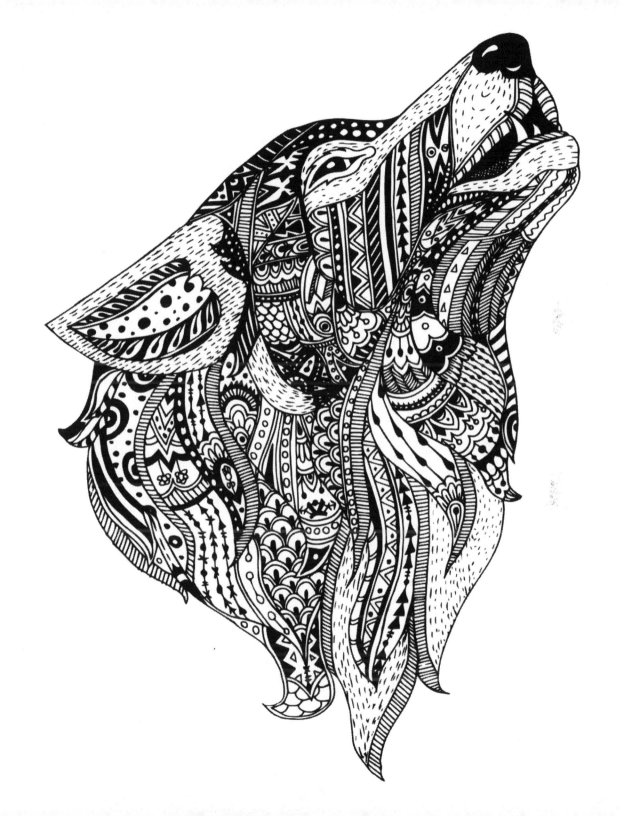

Find more amazing adult coloring books & journals available on *Amazon.com*, *CNandJ.com*, and *InspirationalWares.com*.

The Adult Coloring Book for
Coffee Lovers

Good People Drink Good Beer:
Beer Tasting Notebook

Be Strong and Courageous
Journal for Men

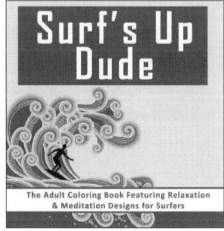

Surf's Up Dude
The Adult Coloring Book Featuring Relaxation &
Meditation Designs for Surfers

Color Test Page

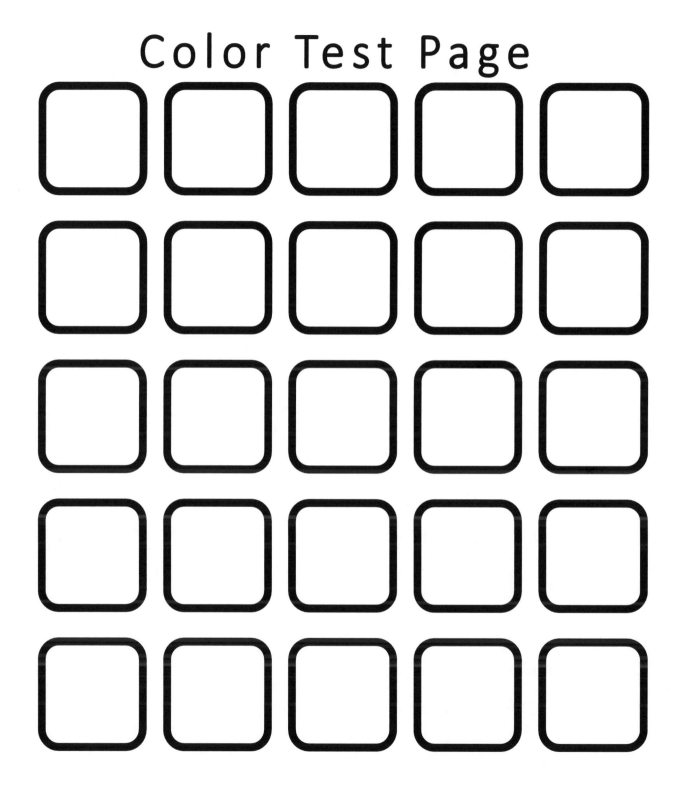

Made in United States
Orlando, FL
25 July 2022